ONE SMALL STEP

USING HABIT STACKING TO IMPROVE YOUR LIFE AND ACHIEVE SUCCESS

I0456198

BY SMART READ.

Free Audiobook

ABOUT SMARTREADS

Choose Smart Reads and get smart every time. Smart Reads sorts through all the best content and condenses the most helpful information into easily digestible chunks.

We design our books to be short, easy to read and highly informative. Leaving you with maximum understanding in the least amount of time.

Smart Reads aims to accelerate the spread of quality information so we've taken the copyright off everything we publish and donate our material directly to the public domain. You can read our uncopyright below.

We believe in paying it forward and donate 5% of our net sales to Pencils of Promise to build schools, train teachers and support child education.

To limit our footprint and restore forests around the globe we are planting a tree for every 10 hardcover books we sell.

Thanks for choosing Smart Reads and helping us help the planet.

Sincerely,

Travis & the Smart Reads Team

TABLE OF CONTENTS

INTRODUCTION

Change is often a challenging and an inevitable force in people's lives. Change can come unexpectedly, or more accurately, unsolicited. It can knock you out of your routine or alter the course of your life in a way you may not consider beneficial. At the same time, there are many instances in which you may wish to spark a change in your current circumstances. But as you know well, it can lead to severe discouragement when you fail to enact the change you seek.

Majority of people don't deal with change very well. Most would rather stick to the "routine" rather than instigate change because it allows them to live a "problem-free" life.

It's a given that the mind likes to produce routines: patterns of daily movement and task managing that occur without substantial effort. Each routine consists of a series of smaller, individual actions that act as milestones in your daily accomplishments.

These are called habits.

Your habits can be good or they can be bad. Regardless, it's likely you are dimly aware of these habits as you go about your business. These habits have become so embedded in your subconscious that they tend to require little to no energy on your part to do.

In fact, it often costs us time and productivity when operating outside of an established routine.

This time and energy cost often deters people from making major life movements all at once. For instance, you know that you should be active for at least an hour a day, it would certainly help relieve back pain, but you don't have an hour all at once to give up. You also know that you should be eating better, but overhauling your diets requires time, research, budgeting, cooking lessons, perhaps a whole new lifestyle altogether. When you apply this concept throughout your life, it boils down to something along the lines of: "I know that I could, but I just don't have the time or energy to make it happen."

To console yourself, you remind yourself that Rome wasn't built in one day. Then eventually you end up abandoning the idea of building Rome altogether.

What this book seeks to teach is, in fact, exactly how Rome was built: over time, building by building—at times, brick by brick.

This principle exists in the modern era and is called "habit stacking." In short, it follows the principle of adding to or consolidating the habits and routines that are already embedded in your day-to-day activities. This prevents mental overload, and reduces the stress of trying to make too many changes all at once.

Habit stacking shifts the responsibility of positive action to your routine, and if executed properly, will allow you to complete tasks no matter what the stress of your situation. After all, at the end of the night, no matter how long or stressful, you still manage to find time to brush your teeth. Without this habit, the impact on your teeth and overall health could be catastrophic, but you don't really think about that. You simply do it.

The goal of habit stacking is to build upon previously existing habits and routines, such as brushing your teeth, in a way that allows important long-term goals to be met by the daily accomplishment of mindless tasks.

Piecing Together a Habit Stacking Routine
Building upon existing habits and crafting a new routine is not something that you usually do intentionally. The nature of your own routines can be

elusive until you take the time to observe and consider them.

Before introducing specific ways and areas of your life in which you can start linking your existing habits, you should establish the fundamental principles that make habit stacking so effective. Understanding the key elements to habit stacking can help ensure that your routines are both achievable and beneficial. Here are eight principles to consider:

I. Habits Should Be Simple
Stress can cripple a routine, and failing to accomplish one goal often prevents you from moving on to the next goal. In a routine, your individual habits should be simple and immediately achievable in and of themselves. Think making the bed, or drinking a glass of water.

II. Keep to the Five-Minute Rule
Remember that the number one deterrent to a person's ability to make a change is time commitment. Keeping habits to five minutes or less is an effective way to structure routines that do not infringe upon obligatory time or free time. To put it into perspective, there are 255 five-minute windows in a day. Building routines of tasks that require less than five-minutes to

complete is less daunting when considering time in windows such as these.

III. Be Complete
Habits should be self-contained, and not open to growth or expansion. Making your bed is a consistently open-and-closed-book task that will keep you moving from one task to the next without risking overdoing it.

IV. Aim for Life Improvement
It goes without saying that you should aim to improve your life and build positive habits, and not destructive or negative habits. You will find that habit stacking improves general areas of your life, and that the success of a routine is dependent upon the energy and wellbeing that you will gain through habit stacking. The less time that a routine takes, the better.

V. Routines Should Take Less Than 30 Minutes
Once a series of tasks are compiled into a routine, you should make sure that the entire routine takes less than 30 minutes. It becomes difficult to maintain a consistent course of action the more that your routine takes out of your time and overall energy. To make routines easily achievable, try reducing the amount of time it will take you to complete all the tasks.

VI. Check it Off the List

Don't waste time during your routine playing a guessing game of what comes next. Routines are meant to be exactly that, routine courses of action that you do not have to mentally prepare for or be 100% intentional to execute. To get into the flow of a new routine, keep a checklist until the routine becomes second nature. As an additional bonus, checking each item off the list creates a feeling of overall accomplishment as you go about your day.

VII. Make Sure the Flow Makes Sense

If you move from grocery shopping to vacuuming your house, you'll need to keep in mind the travel time and transition between tasks that will take time out of your routine. In this case, the time commitment is not feasible. Keep your tasks flowing logically one into the next, like an assembly line of tasks that feed down your routine without you having to switch tracks.

VIII. Make Sure the Routine Fits Your Life

Working with your natural daily cycle and taking advantage of elements of your routine that are already in place can help you build tasks upon previous routines. If you know that you are going to be out and about at a certain time in your day, build your routine around your location. Be conscious of points in your day where you experience high and low energy levels. Completing especially rewarding tasks at the higher energy level points of your day can help you power through the lower energy points.

With all of this in mind, you can build multiple routines into your day and cut through the cluttered, often time-consuming activities that occupy your free time. Instead of dedicating part of your weekend to deep cleaning, you could be doing a quick wipe down of the kitchen after every dinner.

Habit stacking applies most directly to seven general areas of life:
1. Productivity
2. Relationships
3. Finances
4. Organization
5. Spirituality & Mental Health
6. Health & Physical Fitness
7. Leisure

Each chapter in this book will cover one of these areas in depth, with suggestions for how to get started. It is up to you to decide what will work best for you. The routines that you set for yourself will be yours to benefit from, so use this book as a companion guide or springboard for the habits and routines that you put into practice.

Over time, you will experience the benefits of healthy habits without even thinking about the little things you do every day to achieve them.

CHAPTER 1: PRODUCTIVITY

You probably know the feeling of regret that comes after a short pause between tasks turns into a long break between work, which then turns into a wasted hour or more of mindless scrolling through social media feeds. When you feel as though you do not have enough time in a day, you need to address how much of that time is wasted time, because nothing cripples both efficiency and rest like time-killers.

Many of the actions that you can take may seem obvious, but at the same time, it seems obvious that cutting time in front of screens would improve the general quality of life. By adding these small tasks to your daily routine, your productivity will skyrocket, and you will find that your work is greater in both volume and quality.

Here are some tasks that might lead you to a more productive workday.

Stay Hydrated
Most people wait until they are thirsty to drink water, and by that time, water isn't always readily available. This, paired with the caffeinated beverages people usually turn to for liquid assistance, can lead to fatigue, trouble concentrating, and headaches. In the long term, failing to stay hydrated can have negative

effects on your short-term memory, and can begin to alter your mental state.

The general recommendation for how much water you should drink in a day is 8 eight-ounce glasses. Try to fit a glass of water into your morning routine, meals, or work breaks. It will take less than five minutes out of your entire day, and will keep you focused and clear as you go about your business.

Give Your Day Direction
Even if you don't like being kept to a schedule, you should take the time to create a general course of action for your day. It is easy to lose large amounts of time out of your day trying to decide what you should do, and it may also cause you to accomplish a task that isn't time sensitive over a task that has a crucial deadline.

It helps to write your goals for the day in a notebook or journal. Even if you don't reference it during the day, it allows you to lay everything out on a physical space while you process tasks. You might want to assign values to each task, highlighting the tasks that are vital over the tasks that are unimportant. Give yourself an idea of how long you will be working on your larger tasks, and be generous with any timeframes that you set on a project. Most importantly, take only five minutes in the morning to schedule your day, and don't stress over the prospect of what you have on your plate.

Set Yourself Up for Success

With such structured lives; it is nearly impossible for anyone to accomplish every single task they have on their plates every single day. For this reason, it is important to set yourself up for success by selecting a few critical tasks that give you something to focus on and achieve. Completing highly prioritized tasks will make you feel accomplished, even if you are completely unable to get to any of your other tasks.

Depending on how well you prioritize (see above), this task may be a simple matter of choosing the two or three tasks you will accomplish before turning to other, smaller goals. Be realistic, as accomplishing one major goal will make you feel better than accomplishing ten small goals.

Break Down Your Larger Projects

Stress operates on a bell curve, in other words, too little or too much stress and you will not be able to approach a task. If a task seems overwhelming, you are less likely to even begin it, and it can lead to periods of frustration and unnecessary negativity.

Take some time to break down large projects into manageable steps.

This step can fit into any routine, as large projects aren't necessarily things you can complete in one day, or even one week. Take some time in the evening to budget yourself for the next day, or for the next few days. This way, you will understand exactly what you need to do to complete the project, and schedule accordingly.

Find a Productivity Buddy
Motivation is as much an external force as it is an internal force, oftentimes more so. When you get tired or lazy, it is easy for you to shut down your productivity and let your carefully planned-out tasks fall by the wayside. Deadlines do not approach quickly; they suddenly become extremely time-sensitive after a long period of you ignoring them.

Having a productivity buddy is particularly important for tasks without inherent deadlines (client deadline, etc.) This way, you can have someone checking in on you and asking you if you were able to call your parents this week, or finish a chapter of the book you're reading.

Celebrate Your Accomplishments

Burnout is another large factor in overall productivity. Few people can work hard for extended periods of time without receiving some form of affirmation. On a similar note, dreary tasks can seem all the more punishing when they offer no light at the end of the tunnel. Don't let yourself get worn down simply because you aren't taking the time to bask in and acknowledge your successes.

Take some time during your evening routine to plan for victory moments, and scale your rewards to the amount of time and effort that a project takes to complete. You know what you like best, so remember to treat yourself according to your tastes. You might treat yourself to a glass of wine after delivering a presentation at work, or take your friends out to dinner after locking in a new client.

Eliminate Distractions from Work Spaces

This applies to both physical and computer spaces. Clutter and disorganized workspaces can cause stress without realizing the source of distraction. Likewise, you lose a vast amount of time to social media, notifications, television screens, or almost any other source of sound and light. In order to work more effectively, choose locations or create a space where you will not be constantly tuning out distractions just to stay focused.

When it comes to spaces, take a moment to eliminate or organize physical clutter, or work in environments that do not offer distractions. For your computer, this can be as simple as turning off notifications, or as involved as downloading and installing software that block social media and communication sites.

Tune Out Your Surroundings

Sounds can be unpredictable and distracting, and workplaces tend to consist of the same noises that pull us out of focus. To keep yourself in a mental groove, try listening to playlists of ambient, background noise. Each person has different preferences, but most rely upon some form of white noise or a soundscape from nature.

The only way to figure out what works to you is to experiment and discover what does and doesn't work. For some, the hustle and bustle of a coffee shop provides a layer of background warmth that helps them focus. Alternatively, some people like apps that put customizable soundscapes on an infinite loop. If you choose to listen to music, it is important that you choose music without lyrics that you cannot easily recognize. Whatever you find to work for you, have it readily available for whenever you sit down to work.

Do It Sooner Rather than Later

Instead of putting off quick, small tasks because they are unpleasant or unrelated to the task at hand, do everything that comes up that will take you less than two minutes to do. If you find yourself regularly needing to set aside time to accomplish accumulated small tasks, trying becoming active in clearing out small tasks as they crop up.

Review Your Goals Frequently

Working as hard as you can without ever looking up and reassessing the situation can lead to large amounts of precious time and effort spent on the wrong task. If you've ever had to go back and correct your work, then you know how frustrating and time consuming this can be.

Be sure to set aside time in your daily routine to make sure you are on the right track, and that you are making forward progress in whatever assignment you are working on. That way, you can ensure that every minute you spend working on a task is ultimately leading you to completion, and not to correction.

CHAPTER 2: RELATIONSHIPS

Just like the people who comprise them, relationships are often the most sustaining, messy, and exciting parts in people's lives. They also require a considerable amount of effort, and without proactive thought, relationships can be much more difficult than they need to be.

Unfortunately, relationships are usually one of the first things to go when the going gets tough. Spending time with someone can be difficult when you feel as though you do not have any time to spend. Still, relationships benefit from more than just time alone. These simple tasks can help keep your friends close.

Return Missed Messages
Communication is critical in a relationship, and if you miss a call or a text, you owe it to yourself and to the relationship to respond. After all, someone took the time to think about you and send you a message! Taking some time to call or text back will help you feel like you have people who care about you and want to talk.

The best thing to do is check your missed calls and call people back. Phone calls can be time consuming, but they give you a chance to hear about someone else's life, and to share from your own as well. If you don't have time talk, you can let the person know by sending them a text message. You know your friends best, so plan your time accordingly.

Send an Encouraging Text

Knowing someone is thinking of you during an important moment in your life is a wonderful feeling. It is also a feeling that you have the ability to put into others, and it will make you feel good too!

Odds are that you know someone who could use a little encouragement in their day. Think of someone who might be facing an important deadline, test, performance, or other event, and let him or her know you are thinking about them.

Schedule Lunch & Dinner Dates

There is something special that happens when you get to know someone over a plate of food. Whether it is a new relationship, or the deepening of an old one, getting food together is a way to build stronger, healthier relationships.

Putting in a small amount of effort to come up with a time, date, and location for the date will make scheduling the date considerably easier. Additionally, the person that you are trying to connect with will find it much easier to commit to a specific time, and will be less likely to cancel as the date approaches.

Manage Your Social Calendar

Without keeping track of your social commitments, it is easy to forget about one and schedule another on top of it. Don't put yourself in a situation where you are having to scramble to reschedule or cancel on one friend because of your commitment to another. While most may understand, you do not want to continually be playing catch up on commitments you were unable to keep.

This task can be as rigorous as keeping a physical social calendar, or you can track of dates and times on your phone. Whenever you make plans, just remember to block out that time on your calendar, and if you find you've just set aside a time that conflicts with someone else's time, be sure to correct the mistake sooner rather than later.

Be Proactive on Social Media

Today's digital networking can be frustrating for a lot of people, and can be discouraging when you feel as though you do not garner enough interest in your posts or activities. One way to combat the troubles of social media networking is to be proactive in building your own network.

Most social media sites, including Facebook and LinkedIn, have a section that suggests other users you might know. Since people are constantly joining these large-scale networks, you should get into the habit of checking for people that you may know and connecting with them or adding them as a friend. Even if you don't get a response, you will know you took the initiative and put forth the proper effort in the relationship.

Share Your Interests
Making online connections and adding friends is not the most important part of being connected to others. No matter your area of community, be it online or in person, you should be surrounding yourself with friends and colleagues who share the same interests as you. These people will know how to best support you in your goals and aspirations, no matter the length or level of the relationship.

Take a few minutes out of your day to browse through community pages or visit community areas. If you are getting into biking, stop by the local bike shop and get to know someone who also has an interest in biking. It may be strange at first, and you may not immediately connect with each person, but by seeking out others who share your interests, you will quickly garner a community of like-minded individuals who support each other in the same pursuit.

Search for Events Near You
It is easier to make plans with people when there is something going on that draws people in. No matter how large or small your community, there is always some kind of event going on, so do your research and lead a band of people to go to the event and have fun with each other if nothing else.

Search online or visit your local coffee shop to discover things near you. If you live in a city or suburb, you might be surprised at what you'll find if you treat yourself like a tourist in the area. Best of all, most locally hosted events are free to attend, so go and have a fun time simply being out in public with your friends.

Relish Your Personal Time
You are at your best when you do what makes you happy first. By setting apart some time to do what makes you happy, you can ensure that you are bringing the best of yourself to the table in a relationship.

Take some time to reflect upon the things that make you feel good. Whether it be listening to your favorite music, reading a good book, going for a walk, or enjoying a good cup of coffee, take that time to restore yourself and consistently be at your best when meeting with others.

Learn to Empathize with Others
Relationships are never fruitful when they are self-centered. If you want to share in someone's life and impact them, it is important to spend time considering what that person might be going through in their lives. If you have a friend who is going through a hard time, you should be thinking about how best to serve them, and not vice versa.

Take time each day to think through the lives of your friends or family members. Consider what each one is going through and what exactly about a difficult situation might be so difficult. Consider any ways in which you might be able to alleviate that person's grief. Learning to empathize with others is the surest way to building meaningful, long-lasting relationships with others.

Share Something Funny
Throughout the course of a day, you might see something that makes you laugh, or see something that makes you think of someone else. Take the extra

few seconds to send it to that person, or share a funny moment with someone close to you. By extending the moment to someone else, you can brighten someone's day and let them know you are thinking about them.

Get in the habit of following up something funny on social media with the thought of who might best appreciate the reason you are laughing. Odds are, if it made you think of a specific person, that person will enjoy it as much if not more than you did.

Leave a Note
This action has the power to both send someone an encouraging message, and let them know you are thinking about them in a big way. By leaving the note in the path of another person's routine, it can be a pleasant and uplifting surprise in the middle of their day.

The note does not have to be lengthy or thought out, but be sure to place it somewhere that it will be encountered by the other person. A backpack, briefcase, or dashboard would be the type of ideal location. You might be surprised the effect that even a small note can have on the person receiving it.

CHAPTER 3: FINANCES

Contrary to popular belief, the best way to improve your financial situation is not to start making more money. Not only is this philosophy too often unrealistic, but it also fails to address the underlying issue at hand.

Your finances are matters of personal preferences and habits, and improving the situation is not so much about how much money you have as it is about how you direct and command your resources. Developing smart financial habits is the best way to manage debt, save up, and leave a good amount of change in your pocket for personal enjoyment. Try developing some of these habits and see how they can positively impact your financial situation.

Check and Manage Accounts
At any given point in time, you should know how much money is in your bank account. For most, checking on and knowing the balance in a single account is no problem. The reality is that many find it necessary to open more than one account, and this includes open credit lines.

You should get into the habit of checking and managing all of your accounts at least a few times a week. This way, you can ensure that you do not fall behind on payments, and you can prevent overdrawing and unnecessary stress that comes from making payments without knowing how much money is in the account.

Educate Yourself on Personal Finances

Today's world of finances is constantly changing, and it pays to know the state of the economy and how you can maneuver yourself into the best financial position possible. You should always do your research before making significant financial moves, and by reading up on experienced or studied financial advisors, you can avoid costly mistakes and understand the inherent risks of the financial world.

Subscribe to a personal finance magazine, or find a daily column written by a financial advisor you trust. It may take some digging to get started, but once you get into the habit, reading a daily article on finances can be informative, insightful, and relaxing.

Penny Pinch

Keeping track of loose change might feel like a meaningless task, but you would be surprised how much you can save by holding on to quarters and dimes. Keeping a jar of change in your car or your house will provide you with a small reserve of cash to use when the parking meter only accepts quarters, or when you just need a small cash reserve on hand.

Get in the habit of carrying cash around with you, and spending in cash instead of using your card. This way, you will accumulate change over time, and you will be less likely to make spur of the moment purchases. Once you have the change, store it in a jar or a place where you will not be constantly tapping into it.

Track You Daily Expenditures
Most people are unaware of their spending habits, or if they are, it is because their spending habits have significant impact on their overall budget. By writing down what you spend on and how much every day, you will begin to identify trends in how you spend your money. Once those trends are identified, consider their necessity and adjust accordingly.

You can keep track of your daily expenses in a checkbook or notebook, or by holding on to your receipts and writing the total down at the end of each day. Include tax, and if you feel you have extra time, try categorizing your expenditures to get a better overview of your spending habits.

Keep Cash on You

Swiping your debit or credit card becomes a frighteningly automatic process when you don't carry cash regularly. Having physical cash in your wallet can raise your awareness of how much your lunch or purchase is costing you. In addition, some businesses are cash only, and you never want to have to rely on ATMs, if possible.

Get an idea of how much cash you would like to have on you at any given time. You can treat cash as a per diem allotment if you regularly eat out to lunch, or you can budget out a certain amount to always have on hand, and challenge yourself to tap into it as little as possible.

Unsubscribe to Sales Emails

Few people open sales emails with the intentions of making a purchase, but after a few minutes of browsing and exploring all of the different ways to save, you might start to feel like you're losing out on a deal if you don't buy! This is an illusion engineered by marketers to get you to buy their product, and you will save 100% on the purchases that you do not make.

Every advertiser and marketing email subscription must include an unsubscribe button at the bottom, by law. Take a few minutes to unsubscribe to a few mailing lists a day, and eventually, you will find less money lost to impulse buys and less clutter in your inbox.

Use Coupons on Necessities

Common household items are some of the most common items listed on coupon catalogs. At some point, you will need to replenish your laundry detergent, or dish soap, or toothpaste. Necessities are relative to each person, but you should always be taking advantage of the sales on these items. Coupons will allow you to save a few bucks per item, per purchase of that item.

Since most of us prefer not to spend money unnecessarily, get into the habit of browsing and keeping coupons in your wallet or in a separate carrier. It might be a hassle at first, but when you consider the frequency and cost of each necessity you purchase regularly, you might find yourself saving a few hundred bucks a year. Instead of spending that money on detergent, how about a vacation?

Eat Out Less

One of the largest hidden expenses in a person's budget is food. Frequently getting drive through coffee and eating out during the workday can easily cost a few hundred dollars a month. There's nothing wrong with eating out, but packing a lunch or bringing your own coffee to work will save both your wallet and (most likely) your health.

Some people opt to meal prep at the end of each week; in other words, they will cook or prepare everything they will be eating for the rest of the week in one day. If this sounds appealing to you, check out some meal prep sites and take some time each day to plan, otherwise, avoiding eating out can be as simple as bringing a travel mug to work and preparing the next day's lunch the night before.

Free Events
While going out to dinner or the movies is a fun and hassle-free way to enjoy an evening, frequently (or even infrequently) doing so can be costly. Most of us overlook the free events that take place in our communities, but special events can be a great way to have fun while spending little to no cash.

Check a local newspaper or website for upcoming community events, things like free concerts, park gatherings, or market nights. Spend a little time looking outside of your immediate area, and don't be afraid to do a bit of traveling. Driving somewhere an hour away for a free event will still cost you less than dinner and a movie, and odds are that it will be equally rewarding, if not more so.

Be Conscious of Utilities

Your electricity and water usage are billed to you according to how much you use. In some cases, the billing rate gets higher the more you use. If you find yourself having to make an unexpected payment, you might consider dialing back on your electricity and water usage for the month in order to offset your losses.

Regardless of your financial circumstances, you should get into the habit of turning off all lights not currently in use, and limiting the amount of time you spend in the shower. There are many ways to conserve water and limit electricity use, but these two methods in particular will offer you the most immediate changes with the least impact to your quality of life.

Comparison Shop

When you go to buy a car, it pays to do some looking around. With the evolving online world, and an ever-increasing list of producers and designers, you should be extending the principle of comparison-shopping to just about everything you buy. Different brands offer different features and designs that come with different prices and availabilities, so exploring your options can make any purchase more cost-efficient and well-informed.

Any time you go to purchase something, particularly the more costly it is, check out two or three other retailers of the product. Look for quality points and try to get an understanding of how the products differ from one another. Ultimately, you will decide on the one that you feel is best suited for your needs and budget.

CHAPTER 4: ORGANIZATION

Organization is one of the most common and most important traits shared by successful people around the world. Staying organized has benefits beyond a clean and easy to navigate workspace; it allows you to build upon your existing space without having to play catch up on rapidly devolving situations.

The skill will not come easy for everyone, but it does not need to be a time consuming and meticulous endeavor. Staying organized, if only by your own arbitrary standards, will allow you to operate efficiently in both your physical and mental space.

Actively Prevent Buildup

Certain areas get more difficult to deal with over time, for example, the dishes. Instead of waiting until you have a large mess, or something becomes inaccessible, you should get into the habit of actively combatting spaces that get cluttered. This principle extends to mail, trash, laundry, or any area of your home that experiences buildup.

Get into the habit of sorting out these buildup problems right away. Take a minute or two to at least rinse dishes, if not dry and put them away. Never leave trash out, and always throw away junk mail if you know you'll never look at it. You know your lifestyle best, so do what you can to eliminate the unnecessary buildup as it occurs.

Make Your Bed

Getting into this habit early each morning sets a great tone for the rest of the day. It will set your mind into an organizational and productive mode, and will allow you to wind down and get into an already made bed at the end of the night.

Take some time to make your bed as part of your morning routine. It can make your entire room appear more organized, and will give you an immediate sense of order as you set out and face your day.

Keep Countertops Clear

We all set things down on counters absentmindedly, and over time, not clearing off counter spaces can lead to a cluttered, stressful environment. Instead of searching for things in piles, get into the habit of keeping items where they belong.

Pick a surface and return any objects that don't belong on it back to where they belong. This is often the case with clothes, and taking the time to put them away can make them easier to retrieve when you need them. Assign a designated place to keep your phone, wallet, or keys so you never misplace them.

Sell or Give Away Unused Items

Many people hold on to objects or clothing long past the point at which they can or do use them. If the object has value, try selling it online and see if you can make some quick cash off of it. In the case of clothes or other goods, you might consider donating to a thrift store or Goodwill, which will give someone else the opportunity to use something that only takes up space with you.

Designate a bin or storage container to keep unwanted or unused items. Try and be conscious of items in your home that go for more than a few weeks or months without being used. If you aren't interested in giving items away, be on the lookout for sell or trade opportunities in the community.

File Receipts & Paperwork

Loose papers can quickly become annoying, and losing track of a specific loose paper can make it almost impossible to track down. If you have ever needed to return something and been unable to locate the receipt, then you know how important it is to keep track of your purchases.

Keep a folder of receipts and other important paperwork, like tax relevant information or loan payment history. Doing so will prevent unnecessary searching and questioning in the future. This will also drastically reduce the stress of moments where the relevant information becomes necessary information.

Always be Decluttering

Nowadays, clutter exists in both physical and digital mediums. People accumulate clutter by any number of means, and attempting to prevent its existence may not be the best to focus your efforts. Instead, decluttering preemptively and not allowing buildup can lead to more open space, and a general feeling of openness wherever you are working.

If you are dealing with physical clutter, determine how much of it can be thrown out. If it cannot be trashed, try finding a place for it that allows the use of the space that it previously took up. Digital clutter can be a simple matter of moving files to the trashcan, or regularly clearing off your desktop.

Get Rid of Expired Goods

If you don't check your fridge frequently, then odds are you are housing an expired food item. The same can be true for coupons, pantry items, baked goods, or anything that has an expiration date. You are going to want to be in the habit of replenishing your stocks frequently, and never reaching for something only to find it inedible and expired.

Take a few moments every so often in a week to clear out your fridge or pantry. Doing so will allow you to get rid of expired goods, and it will also remind you of exactly what you have in your fridge and pantry to work with.

Develop a "Walking In" Routine
A lot of disorganization occurs the moment you walk into your home, when you are tired and not focused on keeping up the order of your home. Developing a simple routine for where to place your keys, bags, jackets, or anything that you carry on you regularly can help you keep track of the specific objects that you carry with you every day.

Invest in some wall hangers or organizational tools, a side table or corkboard, to keep all of your items in one central location. Once you designate the spots, it will be a simple matter of putting them down there when you enter and picking them up in the same place as you exit.

CHAPTER 5: SPIRITUALITY & MENTAL HEALTH

Your mind is the most powerful tool you have at your disposal, and nothing will make you more aware of this fact than the times that you feel it is turned against you. Keeping yourself mentally healthy, be that through spiritual practice or through general exercises in wellbeing, will allow you to approach the world around you with a more positive and meaningful attitude.

Have Positive Thoughts

Although it may seem redundant and cheesy, simply vocalizing or having positive thoughts can improve your overall mood and set your day off to a strong start. Telling yourself you are loved and valued, in control of your life, or that you are going to be successful that day will set you down the path to making those words a reality.

There is no use dwelling on negative thoughts, or destructive thoughts that hinder your ability to feel good about yourself and accomplish your goals. Instead, get in the habit of encouraging yourself and thinking highly about yourself. Whatever you tell yourself is ultimately the truth that you are going to hear.

Remember Things You Are Thankful For

Thankfulness is a matter of perspective, and being in a constant state of thankfulness will eliminate any feelings of pride, resentment, frustration, and apathy you might experience throughout the day.

Practicing writing down what you are thankful can put you in a more positive frame of mind. If you become thankful for the position you are in, you will be all the more happy for being there. So many people try to derive self-worth and accomplishment in reference to others or to unrealistic goals, but simply being thankful for the day and your health can make you feel lucky and positive about everything that you have going for you.

Put on a Song You Love

Music can cleanse your body and soul, and resonate with your innermost feelings in a way that no other medium can. Music can make you think of happier times, can make you feel understood and valued, and can influence your mood for the better or worse. In any case, music is a powerful tool for mood and mental being.

Keep a few playlists compiled to suit your specific preferences. Happy music isn't for everyone, sometimes, it's the music that says how you feel better than you could that allows you to shift your perspectives on the day and the world around you.

Go Experience the Outdoors

Nature has proven time and time again to be an unbelievably beneficial experience for individuals. Being in the sunlight, breathing in the fresh air, and experiencing the openness and quiet of the outdoors can radically refresh you, and all you need to do is be there.

Even if you do not have time to regularly hike or become an outdoors sportsman, you can eat your breakfast outside, go for a walk in the park, or spend some time taking care of a small garden. As long as you are enjoying the sights, sounds, and smells of the world around you, you are participating in nature's daily beat.

Enjoy a Warm Beverage

Coffee and tea can be extremely relaxing mid-day pleasures, and it should be noted that many countries around the world enjoy a "tea time" or beverage oriented leisure hour. Enjoying these breaks and sipping on a tea or coffee that you enjoy without any pressure of consuming can be an incredibly rewarding experience.

Making your own tea or coffee is simple, and can be learned in less than five minutes! Once you have a coffee or tea preparation system of choice, just get into the habit of treating yourself to a cup every day.

Meditate

There are a lot of stigmas regarding meditation, but at its core, the act of meditating is simply focusing on one object, typically breathing, without allowing other thoughts to occupy your mind and distract you. The goal is not so much to empty your mind as it is to strengthen and discipline your mind against random thoughts or distractions.

Meditation does not need to be an excessive endeavor; it can be a five-minute exercise in the morning that gets you focused and in control of your mind. If you particularly enjoy it, you can extend it to take up a larger amount of your day, but the benefits of meditation can be experienced with only a few minutes of concentration.

Serve Others

Being self-centered and focused only on the benefits that you enjoy out of your own efforts has proven to be negative in the long term. Solely operating with your own benefit in mind leads to a sense of isolation, loneliness, stinginess, defensiveness, and apathy in your life.

Going out of your way to serve others will create a sense of community, shared life-experience, and meaningfulness in life. This is especially true when others express their appreciation for you, which will boost your sense of self-worth and appreciation for the people around you.

Seek Inspiration
The world is a wonderful place, and you never know when a story or passage will jump out at you and challenge you into appreciating the world around you in a new and powerful way. Seeking inspiration does not have to be religious or historical, it can be in the daily lives of the people around you, or an event that causes you to be proud of yourself and others.

Inspiration is everywhere, and finding inspiration is a matter of connecting yourself to the stories of the people and places that interest you. Try to look for quotes outside of the mainstream, and read something that challenges you as well as inspires you.

Keep a Journal
Writing your thoughts out can be one of the most powerful exercises in understanding yourself and

understanding the way that you perceive the world around you. Allow yourself to have each thought, and only correct or judge yourself once you have taken a large enough step back to determine the kind of person that you would like to be mentally.

You are the only one who can truly understand yourself, and becoming the person that you would like to be is difficult when who you want to be is constantly being affected by who you are right now. Simply writing to yourself can be a way of passively shaping yourself into the person that you aspire to be like, and after a while, you will notice a marked improvement in your mental state.

CHAPTER 6: HEALTH & PHYSICAL FITNESS

Exercise is an endeavor that will require more than five or ten minutes a day to build upon. While the following tasks are not necessarily geared towards improving your cardio or overall fitness, they can ensure you are doing everything else you can to set yourself up for success as you work towards achieving a better physical state.

Try adopting some of these habits as ways to supplement your physical fitness routines, and remember that even working out can benefit from a streamlined routine and mentality.

Weigh Yourself Daily
If you have a target weight that you would like to reach, then weighing yourself every day can help you stay focused on your goals. This time is not meant to discourage you, and if you are doing it right, you should be losing weight slowly over time, and not dropping pounds quickly.

Use this time to reflect on all of the things that you are going to do that day to work your way to your target weight, and understand that your weight will fluctuate depending on how much water weight you are carrying. Try and weigh yourself at a specific time of day, usually mornings, for more consistent results.

Keep Track of Your Diet
You should be aware of what you are putting into your body at all times, and keeping a journal allows you to see how maybe that splurge you took this week was one of four splurges that are contributing to an overall trend.

In order to lose weight and keep it off, you need to be making a lifestyle change. Record all of your snacking and drinks, and take some time to review points of your diet that are not necessary, like that midnight snack, or mid-day fountain drink.

Invest in a Jump Rope
This is an easy piece of exercise equipment to have around the house. It is an excellent cardio tool, and does not require any time to set up or put away. It serves well as a warm up, it's portable, and it is significantly less involved than jogging or traditional calisthenics.

Get into the habit of doing a quick session in the mornings, and challenge yourself to a quicker pace, never stopping between jumps. You don't have to go overboard, but pairing jump rope with music and getting into it can be an excellent way to start your day.

Take Your Vitamins
Most of us require more vitamins than naturally occur in our diets. These vitamins can boost immune systems and provide your body with nutrients that increase alertness and overall energy.

Buying vitamins will be the most difficult part of getting into this habit. This task will take less than one minute out of each day, but the benefits can be incredibly rewarding depending on how little of the specific vitamin occurs in your natural diet.

Snack Throughout the Day
Although the standard for American culture is three square meals a day, research indicates that eating smaller portions throughout the day, beginning with a larger breakfast, can keep you more energized throughout the day, without losing energy halfway through.

Get into the habit of packing a few snacks, especially long burning fuel such as nuts and dried fruits, so that you can keep hunger at bay and be energized throughout the day. If you do this right, you can avoid making a large dinner each night, which has been shown to be less beneficial than a smaller meal during the evening.

Stretch or Do Yoga
Your body will experience many benefits from stretching each morning, and you do not need to get into yoga (although, it does help) to experience the increased energy, blood flow, coordination, and decreased tension that stretching brings.

Taking five minutes or less to perform a series of basic stretches can make you feel more awake and more prepared to face the day. If you shower in the morning, add this task in immediately afterwards. Keeping the process slow-paced and relaxed will ensure that you reap the maximum benefits for both your physical and mental wellbeing.

Keep Yourself Groomed
Staying clean and fresh is as physically beneficial as it is mental. The mantra of "look good, feel good, do good" is factual. You will rise to the occasion and take life as it comes far better if you feel clean, healthy, and confident.

Develop good hygiene and get into the habit of showering, shaving, doing your hair, and anything you feel compelled to do. This will allow you to step out into each day feeling healthy and ready to face the day.

Keep Your Kitchen Clean

The kitchen is where you prepare most of the food that goes into your body. Not taking the time to keep it properly sanitary can lead to health problems down the line for both you and your family.

There are a number of different things you can do to keep your kitchen clean, and while this technically falls under the category of organization, cleanliness, in this case can have direct repercussions on your physical health.

Check Your Steps

A lot of people have been getting into monitoring their steps each day, and challenging their friends to daily step competitions. You don't need a smart watch to participate; your smart phone or an app will keep track of your steps just as well.

Download a step counting app and find some friends to encourage you to move around more. You will find yourself taking opportunities to walk around just a little more each day, until you are regularly in the habit of walking around instead of trying to think of ways not to get up.

Choose Healthy Food for Your Gut

Many recent studies have linked poor mental health to gut-related problems, and whether or not you believe the studies, it stands to reason that you should be putting healthy, wholesome food into your body.

Foods that make you feel heavy and bloated will affect your physical abilities and performance throughout the day. Put food into your body that is rich in proteins and calories, and absent of sugars and fats. Fruits and vegetables give your body the most long-term energy, allowing you to keep ticking long past the lunch hour.

CHAPTER 7: LEISURE

Your leisure time is perhaps the most important part of our lives. How you choose to spend the time that is not obligated or strenuous will determine your overall growth and trajectory as individuals.

Instead of draining the most valuable time you have with mindless or unfulfilling activities, try some of these activities out and see if you experience an improvement in your overall quality of life.

Go Outside

There's a reason you've heard this one over and over again. It cannot be overstated; the outdoors and spending time in the sunlight are critical to your overall wellbeing. The more time you spend outside, the more mental and physical benefits you will experience.

Get in the habit of going outside with the free time that you have. It can be a walk through the city, a walk through a garden, or sitting on a bench in the park. Going outside and spending some time in natural sunlight will do you wonders.

Read a Few Pages of a Novel
Regularly reading is a mental exercise that builds concentration and helps to combat age-related mental deterioration. Books can increase your understanding of the world around you, or offer you a temporary distraction from it. Spending a few minutes a day with a good book can relieve stress and has been linked to sleep and blood pressure related benefits.

If you don't read regularly, find a book you might be interested and dedicate five minutes a day to reading through the story. Non-fiction can be a better route for short reading sessions, but anything you will read and enjoy is the way to go.

Be Aware of World Events
Most people find the news depressing or overwhelming, and while this certainly can be true, you might want to consider the fact that not being aware of world events gives you limited to no ability to participate in it.

Take some time each day to follow the daily news, even if only to be aware of headlines. Pursue the subjects that interest you, but be conscientious of the source of your news and take some time to think through issues and events on your own. Your goal should be to spend a small bit of each day attempting to be a well informed citizen, as all of your actions throughout the day affect your culture and community if even in the smallest of ways.

Watch a TED Talk of Thought-Provoking Video

There is a lot of mindless entertainment on television, and while these do offer a sort of escape or drama for us to participate in, there are thought provoking and innovative ideas being spread all around the world. TED is a purveyor of such videos, and there are many other sources of interesting information you can pursue.

You can find TED talks online or through the app store, and it is more than likely you have stumbled upon such videos on your news feed. Limit yourself to one video at a time, and dedicate part of this time to thinking about the ideas that are being presented to you. As information and informative as these videos may be, simply watching them does not always translate to understanding or retaining them.

Learn a New Language

There are many apps on the market that promote the learning of a new language by spending only a few minutes a day immersing yourself in the language. Duolingo and Memrise are two such examples, and if you've ever thought about learning a new language, the education has never been more accessible.

Download a language-learning app and set a daily goal of five minutes to learning a new language. Although it seems like such a small amount of time to be immersed in something as challenging as learning a new language, this small amount of time built up over time will lead to comprehension, to working proficiency, to fluency.

Listen to New Music
A lot of people get wrapped up in their own top ten, and rarely branch out and actively seek out new music. If you find yourself humming the same old tunes, try seeking out new music. This is a great way to get connected to something new, and to introduce a fresh and exciting voice into your life.

Music does not always have to be preference based. Try seeking out music from other genres, things that you don't ordinarily encounter, or new and upcoming musical artists. No matter what you choose to listen to, when you find something that you like, enjoy it and share it with a friend!

Find a Hobby

In today's primarily digital world, a lot of people don't get the chance to use their hands as much as they might like. If you find yourself sitting in front of a screen or operating in a sales / customer service capacity for a majority of your day, consider picking up a hobby that will allow you to work with your hands.

Woodworking, an instrument, crafts, or DIY projects are all great options for anyone looking to get hands on and technical. Like anything that you pursue, cultivate the skills required by studying up on it and doing your research, then follow through and invest a little time and money into it. Even if you only pursue something as a hobby, making something instead of buying it can be surprisingly rewarding.

Try Something New
While the focus of this book is on routines and how to build habits, you should know that the way to introduce excitement into your life is by breaking those hard-won routines. Getting outside of your comfort zone and exploring something totally new can be incredibly exciting and scary. But the rewards of branching out and discovering new things is one of the greatest joys of life.

The options are endless. Try a new food or beverage, travel to a new place, talk to a new person, or do something unexpected. Never limit yourself to your own definitions of what it means to be you: saying that you are not "outdoorsy" should be a challenge to yourself to get out there and have fun.

CONCLUSION

Every one of these tasks requires five minutes or less. Not all of them will be for you, but the ones that are have the potential to drastically improve your quality of life, without demanding or adding to your current stress level.

Before you undergo the task of stacking your habits into a new, streamlined routine, take some time to reflect on how important each of the seven areas of life covered in this e-book are to you. You will only benefit and put effort into those areas so long as they are important, fulfilling, and worthwhile. Ultimately, each area contributes to your holistic wellbeing, and if you find yourself with extra time and seeking a more rewarding life experience, try branching out and focusing on an area of life that you did not previously consider crucial. After all, if you were to master the art of productivity, it would not matter if you didn't maintain relationships or take leisure time.

Now that you have some ideas for how to get started, don't be afraid to come up with your own. If you have habits or routines unique to you, don't be afraid to experiment and come up with ways to further streamline your day. Remember the rules for developing good habits, don't try to do too much, and keep going until you aren't even aware of all of the ways that you have improved your life.

THANKS FOR READING

We really hope you enjoyed this book. If you found this material helpful feel free to share it with friends. You can also help others find it by leaving a review where you purchased the book. Your feedback will help us continue to write books you love.

The Smart Reads library is growing by the day! Make sure and check out the other wonderful books in our catalog. We would love to hear which books are your favorite.

Visit:
www.smartreads.co/freebooks
to receive Smart Reads books for FREE

Check us out on Instagram:
www.instagram.com/smart_readers
@smart_readers

Don't forget your 2 FREE audiobooks.
Use this link www.audibletrial.com/Travis to claim
your 2 FREE Books.

SMART READS ORIGINS

Smart Reads was born out of the desire to find the best information fast without having to wade through the sheer volume of fluff available online. Smart Reads combs through massive amounts of knowledge compiles the best into quick to read books on a variety of subjects.

We consider ourselves Smart Readers, not dummies. We know reading is smart. We're self taught. We like to learn a TON about a WIDE variety of topics. We have developed a love for books and we find intelligence attractive.

We found that each new topic we tried to learn about started with the challenge of finding the pieces of the puzzle that mattered most. It becomes a treasure hunt rather than an education.

Smart Reads wants to find the best of the best information for you. To condense it into a package that you can consume in an hour or less. So you can read more books about more topics in less time.

OUR MISSION

Smart Reads aims to accelerate the availability of useful information and will publish a high quality book on every major topic on amazon.

Smart Reads hopes to remove barriers to sharing by taking the copyright off everything we publish and donating it to the public domain. We hope other publishers and authors will follow our example.

Our goal is to donate $1,000,000 or more by 2020 to build over 2,000 schools by giving 5% of our net profit to Pencils of Promise.

We want to restore forests around the globe by planting a tree for every 10 physical books we sell and hope to plant over 100,000 trees by 2020.

Doesn't it feel good knowing that by educating yourself you are helping the world be a better place? We think so too…

Thanks for helping us help the world. You Smart Reader you…

Travis and the Smart Reads Team

WHY I STARTED SMART READS

Every time I wanted to learn about something new I'd have to buy 20 books on the topic and spend way too long sorting through them and reading them all until I arrived at the big picture. Until I had enough perspectives to know who was just guessing, who was uninformed and who had stumbled upon something remarkable.

I wished someone else could just go in and figure that out for me and tell me what matters. That's how smart reads was born. I want smart reads to be a company that does all that research up front. Sorts through all the content that is available on each topic and pulls out the most up to date complete understanding, then have people smarter than me package the best wisdom in an easy to understand way in the least amount of words possible.

For example, I got a new puppy so I wanted to learn about dog training. I bought 14 different books about dog training and by the time I got through the first 5 and finally started getting the big picture on the best way to train my puppy she had grown up into a dog.

Yeah she's well behaved. She doesn't poop in the house. I can get her to sit and come when I call. But what if someone else went in and read all those books for me, found the underlying themes and picked out the best information that would give me the big picture and get me right to the point. And I'd only have to read one book instead of 15.

That would be amazing. I would save time. And maybe my dog would be rolling over, cleaning up after my kids and doing the dishes by now. That my friend, is the reason I started smart reads. Because I wanted a company I can trust to deliver me the best information in an easy to understand way that I can digest in under an hour. Because dog training is one of many subjects I want to master.

The quicker I can learn a wide variety of topics the sooner that information can begin playing a role in shaping my future. And none of us knows how long that future will be. So why not do everything we can to make the best of it and consume a ton of knowledge. And I figured all the better if I can also make a positive difference in the world.

That's why we're also building schools, planting trees and challenging ideas about copyright's place in today's world. Because as a company we have to be doing everything we can to support the ecosystem that gives us all these beautiful places to read our books. Thanks for reading.

Travis

Customers Who Bought This Customers Who Bought This Book Also Bought

Habits of Power: 101 Habits and Lessons Every Great Leader and Icon Used to Achieve Success in their Life

The Art of Coaching: How to Explain Clearly and Become a Good Leader

Change Your Habits in Just Five Minutes A Day: Create Routines and Habits That Will Stick and Change Your Life

Mastering Your Time: Learn How Successful People Enhance Productivity, Beat Procrastination and Do More in Less Time

Overcoming Procrastination: Proven Strategies on How To Improve Focus, Get Things Done and Achieve Your Goals

Unlocking Potential: Master the Laws of Leadership

Reinvent Yourself: Become Instantly Likable, Captivate Anyone in Seconds and Always Know What To Say

Reading Made Easy: Learn Effortless Reading and Achieve Extraordinary Results